Knees in The Garden

KNEES IN THE GARDEN

Christina D. Rodriguez

QUERENCIA

Querencia Press, LLC
Chicago, Illinois

QUERENCIA PRESS

© Copyright 2023
Christina D. Rodriguez

ISBN 978 1 959118 10 7

www.querenciapress.com

First Published in 2023

Querencia Press, LLC
Chicago, IL

Printed & Bound in the United States of America

CONTENTS

Preface

The desire to be loved...

I was once told that I have a melancholy way about life. Maybe it comes from the trauma of a childhood that was filled with rejection by my peers because of my appearance or the lack of love between my parents and their lack of ability to walk away from something that wasn't working sooner. Witnessing hurt, witnessing bad decisions, witnessing cruelty without thought. In front of me, in the flesh, love was received cautiously.

My first safe love was music. I didn't always have a lot, but I was always surrounded by ways to hear music. My most precious gift was a Sony Walkman that I received at the age of six. My mom, often listening to the oldies station, set my radio there. Curiously, as any six-year-old would do, I wandered away to another point of the dial. CD 101.9, the smooth jazz station of New York. It was the first kind of love that wasn't cautious. I love all types of music, but smooth jazz takes me to a place I was not able to describe succinctly until my late twenties, when my pen became my ultimate instrument and way to love.

I started writing poems at the age of thirteen. I was already a vivacious reader and wrote plenty of diary entries, love notes to undeserving little boys and even silly short stories that won a prize or two. But with poetry, I could roll everything into one perfect (or at least perfect to me) poem and maybe someone would fall madly in love with my words, my wit, my confessions...with me. I wanted to be seen in the way listening to music made me feel, in the way reading books transformed me to some place safe. I wanted to be swept away and left breathless, where all the good and the bad was worth it for this moment of love. I wanted what my parents didn't always show each other. I wanted acceptance from all those around me. I wanted to be seen and loved without caution.

As I've grown into a woman, I've learned that any type of love is not about being seen by others, but how you learn to see yourself, despite all the ways the world tells us it's only the external that counts. To give and receive love is an effort between you and those who you choose to exchange love with. The journey to that isn't easy. Sometimes it's a bit melancholy or awkward, and it definitely helps to have some wit and creativity along the way. As I continued to learn about writing and the craft of poetry, I wrote my way into love.

Why I wrote this book is best described in my artist statement, the whole reason I create:

"I am a lover of language and a worshiper of making people into altars. I started writing as a way to talk about living with a broken heart, navigating through rejection of my body in many forms. As a writer, I want to make space for the sacred and the mundane, hoping that it transcends into a moment that stays with others, bridging the gap of constant loneliness."

That moment is a stream of consciousness that knocks the reader into a state of breathlessness. You know that feeling. You don't know where your lungs have gone and your heart walked out the door, in praise, seconds before. You sit in a state of trembling and wonderment, trying to figure out what your life was before you read these words. Your body is singing in praise, in astonishment. Sometimes the feeling is so intense that you have to stop and close your eyes to bring yourself back into your skin. As a poet, this is the ultimate achievement—the art, the state of breathlessness.

If I leave you, the reader, fulfilled in a moment of breathlessness, that's all I need. A moment to be seen and loved without caution.

Thank you.

"I love you, the way I love you, the way I can love you."

To all the altars I've created through the bodies of the world,
I saw your limitations, but you were an endless sky when you
landed
on my chest.

Thank you for leaving your mark.

It will help me make mine.

"To fall in love is to create a religion that has a fallible God."

— Jorge Luis Borges

Daily Bread

Today let me
give you crumbles

weeping
(v.)
sprig of wounds
poured
from the spine
of my palms

clamoring
(v.)
draft of tender
contracting
in the back
of my throat

housing
(n.)
jar held
squarely
in the base
of my lungs

whistling
(adj.)
color of
your sheets
after
memories have
gone damp
and
astray

The Echo

I.

It was a Sunday
morning, chasing
the 6 train till
I found your limbs
dangling from
my mouth.

II.

My chest never settles
until minutes after
three in the after-
noon, when you are
tucked neatly under
phone wire and bed
bugs, listening for
the buzz of immigrant
drivers.

III.

Let me sell you
the moon under
the typeface of
weathered floorboards
behind La Casa Azul.
On the anniversary
of chinned-pulled
kisses, I attempt
to repair my veins
in the breeze of
paper lantern peacocks.

Heartcode (Censored)

I walk
in
pulsating
hollowness,
pretending
to
breathe in
morse code,
-...
.
.-..

...-
.
-..
breaking
against
lung cages
day and night
as if
my body only
knew one
symphony
to
be smeared
onto the
camera-eye.
[...]

Confessions

confessions?
        no darling...

i know better than that.

        i taught aesop how to tell fables.

you would have to hold those
delicious lips to my temple
to shake the truth from me.

i'm a hell of a tart in the bed
we will never share.
lay those eyes on me and i'll confess

what fools already know:

        i want you, brilliantly.

20

Repent

When the Devil's gone
international and God asks
for a napkin, you open
your palms like the world is
a mass—waiting for parts
of his body to be
placed on your skin.

The slow
smile of an accident
quickly falls beneath
your tongue,
held parts of
the Beloved in your mouth
like a benediction.

Months later,
you still taste
the earth shattered
in the outfall of your ocean
ridden body that tries
to forget time, waiting
for the wind
to pass along
a 'peace be with you'—
where kryptonite
does not
weaken you
to the knees

wiping your mouth
clean of declarations
at night to pray:

Dear God,
today I wrote
a poem.

I saved it
on a napkin
for you after the
Devil tore my dreams
in two
scattering forgiveness
across your
sky

...Now, can I
be saved?

Holy

We are a book
of crooked spine
thick with journey,
testimony of sun-
light and soft caress.

The day I outlined
your eyes as prayer
marked the beginning
of a story that shakes
as we kneel deeper
into genesis.

We
stop, start
dive, scrap,
regenerate

origin
with the lines
of our palms
as we let denial fall
away from
our lips.

Truth
can be found
in the flick
of a wrist

over puckered
and smeared.

I told God
Let me keep
track with the push
of a button.

Your job
is to make sure
we stay in
print

pressed against
blooming flowers,
a picnic
of laughter
to be married
with tears,
raising
an army
of our own
scraped knees;

our own
enchiridion
of love.

Waxing Sienna

Full, pale belly
in the
haze of idle
thoughts
—a child
with the brilliance
of her mother
splashed into
creation
by the vulnerability
of her father.

They once dreamed
of her
sparingly,
under
the damp grass
of clandestine
pulling of
jeans to ankles,

scraping
fingernails
into clumps
of dirt,

burning
a half-moon
into a womb
falling fast
into infatuation,
now waxing
and dripping
into a whirl
of
pumping
hips, burnt
and
stained of
Sienna.

The Wane of Her

We flew
above
the sky's climax,
surrounded by electric
bursts of star-riddled
freckles of Mother
Earth.

My descent into her
clouded flesh
landed me
in the heart of
fires.

A little more
to the left
and we both
could light
up
your hands.

Worship

She shimmered
      graceless
songbirds dangling
from her chin;
a prayer   looped
in fortitude,
taunt and dainty
on hipbone.

Fields of Beloved Blame

All dirt roads pave to me,
a halogen bulb broken in
between stalks of barbican
flesh and holes puckered
in a dying sky, your mouth
ready to smear my sterling.

The truth about poems

Little girl
with the little book
of flowery poems
and love—

unplug sugar rhymes
from your tongue.

Give her a pot
to boil her teeth.

There's no way
to coat transgressions
of thought as
they sit with you
in the edges
of dark.

You laid with
Midas in the delusion
of New York,
as if monkeys and slides
were only left in
the playground
of the golden days.

Eventually
you have to backpack
back to the cornfields,
frequency haywire
in a tango of stained
Bukowski and inherent
vice, a harbor
left empty longer
than the Williamsburg
bridge.

How long can you
hold the compass
pointing towards east
when anything can
make it go south?

Poetry books are
never fairytales;

they're maps of
spoilt devotion.

Mujer of Combustible Living

She is a barrel of the moment, mujer of combustible living.
She belongs to the incandescent curiosity of catechismal tongues,
who scrape layer after layer with each flutter.
Quieren su chispa, her warmth spun in
cloaked denial, because they can't clasp
the diaphanous instant of her,
mujer of combustible living,
coming alive under
their refused
languishing.

mother never told me stories

about men like him, the kind
who dangle your glories
dangerously enshrined.

he'll hammer charm into your heart
between plots to steal motel
flat screens, reluctance teased apart,
cunnilingus done well

in the form of cigarette stained
tongues and ghosts fingered in
your stubborn little mouth, restrained
for you to receive sin,

avalanched down your pretty new
panties to match the tears he'll
leave on the Queens-bound R, a slew
of brined-craze cheeks feel.

Loose

To lovers on the train who devour each other for one stop.

I see her hunger
to be your universe
as you hold her spine
like a trigger
gone loose.

I've seen a house
of cards stand
longer than
her ribcage
as you trail
kisses on her
landmine limbs.

Be careful love,
she has a habit of
falling into flames
and you are burning
bright, biting
into shoulder
blades

that tremble
as if you will
scar and
stay.

Red, Red Rose

Stuck to thighs,
like thorns
splintered in
the pad of
your flesh,
my lips cling
to soft
apexes of the
center region
of demise.

atoms apace
with anticipation
to the arrival
of mouth
on the edge of
the pistol
my mother
always told me
would disquiet
my equanimity,

annexed
when my tongue
splays across
its fleshy rim,
a blooming, sticky

petal fallen
upon the tip
of a barrel,
looking
to pour

its
bloody
need
for the pistol's
arrival
in ruby
windpipes
and
desire for
its steamy
cool body

to do something
other than
wound
the
bosom
its opaque
bullets come
so dangerously
near.

Daughters of Tamar

You were the palms of God
until your lips ducked
out of sight, in the cleft
of my pithy ardor
where your breath reduced me
to burnt knees, crossed.

Draped in torn
sackcloth, I bewail the ash
smeared across the last
place your lips
touched, face buried
in silence.

Prize: Fat Girl

Your body is a small-town trophy for the around-the-way boys who didn't get a taste the first time around. In the city that never sleeps with fat girls in public, you're the cocky boys' secret fetish. The ones who know their smile makes you blush, who hold the body of gods, who flex their charm to your quivering knees. They slide into private screens with proposals of covert ecstasy, booking late-night appointments after the buses stop running. They offer their bodies with the arrogance of holy grail, thinking theirs is the only one on your altar.

These are the boys who never tell you, *You're pretty*. They comment on the depth of your throat, the strength of your knees, the dew between your thighs. They never ask *how was your day*, they hardly answer to *how was yours*. They have a sixth sense in knowing when you are over their games and pop up when you are doing just fine. These boys are in it for the chase, to quell a curiosity of *Do big girls do it better? A big girl is a freak.*

They won't be your friend in the light, but they know how to turn on the denial in your body as you attempt to dig for substance and connect. These boys are conquer-bines, looking to feed their egos with a woman they would never be able to keep up with, in a body that matches the depth of her heart. Have her and she's the Plan B on the shelf—an ornament he'll leave with a shallow engraving you'll trace as another notch on the belt you let him slip off.

Goddess

i.

I AM A GODDESS!

that's right, i am
CHRIST-IN-A world
of poetry

twirling in that red dress
Kim screams about in
what do women want

i am fierce, darling
i am magic
i am hips and thighs
spread across his
face on a Sunday morning

he worships me,
these chaotic bird
nest curls,
these heavy mystic
orbs rolled between his fingers

i am the page he ripped out
of a volume of Neruda
to keep in the seams
of wallets and jeans

i jingle jingle, jingle it baby
—fire, belly-deep
giggles from pretty lips
puckered
in secrets no man
can keep.

ii.

warrior wrapped in
ink spotted sheets,
tapping away
wisdom in a glass
of wine

tilt back and
let me glide
down the open
spine of your
tongue

let me burst
in your mouth,
the red folds
of my dress
swishing past
your ears.

today, you'll
hear the earth
laugh sweet.

Morning Rivers

morning rivers
gush with the scent
of secrets, full of epistles
you fill on your tongue,
and trace along your fingers.

during the highest
of waves, you pop
fleshy tips
laced
with my taste
between my lips.

i taste confessions
backward, eagerly reclaiming
every syllable you steal
as you sharpen your own
tales between my thighs.

we are both addicted
to the scent of arrival.

i kiss you for hours
to continue,
to taste
the moments
i flickered
with
life.

Good girls aren't supposed to beg for water

Have you ever wanted to say something inappropriate?
Where your mouth itches like burnt sun,
when your fingers constantly dance tap
to every person you have loved and teared over?

You constantly fight oxygen from forming words
that house a legion of pounding emotions,
knowing you will be, you are the screaming
woman on the other side of the door,
where silence pretends you're not there.

Every day I want to tell you, *I miss your skin.*
Your arms smooth, your shaking hands.
I never got to kiss your shaking hands.
My brain is in a constant loop of *I love you*
packed neatly in cross-legged politeness of *How do you do?*

Good girls aren't supposed to beg for water.
We are supposed to wait with blindfolds for flowers
to pass across our knuckles, for armor to get down
on one knee and cup devotion upon our cheeks.

But I am not good. I am loving. I am kind.
But I am not good. I've watched duplicates of
my heartbeat swirl down drains and thrown
the completely devoted from my altar.

I tell you *I love you* and you say, *Okay.*
You say, *Okay.* yet every day I want
to tell you, *I miss your skin, your shaking hands.*
I want to be openly clandestine in your shower,
in city parks, on the train platform, watching coming storms.

Feed me burnt sun, if you can't give me water.
Tell me you'll think about it, that you've thought about it.

Tell me if I am being inappropriate. Tell me to go.
Tell me to go scratch my itch somewhere else and come back
friendly.

Or tell me, *Wait. I'm not ready, but wait.*
There's a chance, but wait. Tell me *I miss your skin,*
but I have to find a way to love mine.

I can wait in the pews, until you invite me to the altar.
I've never been the girl to deny even dirty water.

The Scapegoat

Her quietness is a witness;
permission for others to:

Lie
Brag
Judge
Gossip
Backstab
Cry

in her presence as if she was confession,

fallen veils gathered to scrapbook
—held gently in her hands
as if they were her own burdens.

Can being a secret keeper transform you
into mirrors, reflecting transgression
after transgression until you become
the worst parts of others?

Their flaws become her flaws
—she is now the perfect platform
for punishment, where forgiveness
is asked of her, but hardly given.

Her quietness is the perfect victim;
permission for others to groom
their faults as her own.

The perfect way to push her
to the edge with their sudden
goodbye.

Here

Places that make you feel
like a loner failure?

Mark *here*.

Places you are broken?

Mark *here*, *here*, and right *here*.

Places where you can't pass go?

Mark *here* again.

Places you apologize
for being yourself?

You guessed it,
put a mark right *here*!

If you stay *here*,
you drown.

If you come back *here*,
no one notices
you were gone.

You have fought to be
in one place for so long
you don't realize
it all starts *here*.

Who you are to the world
is *here*.
Who you say you are
is *here*.

Who people believe you are
is *here.*
Who you pretend to be
is *here.*
Who you love
is *here.*
Who you hate
is *here.*
Who betrays you
is *here.*
Everything in your world
is *here.*

Whether it's
real,
perceived,
or made up,
you can't deny
it's all *here.*

One day,
you are somebody.
The next,
just a name on a list.

Algorithms show
you can make noise
five times a day and
someone can hear
everyone but you

as you ride on
the waves of *here.*

Pink Tuesday

You're not going
to have too many
successes,

said Jesus.

I remember this,
subliminally messaged
to me during one of
those mundane trips

when obligation to
life was one of those
things to do
on a dusky Tuesday
evening.

No surprise there,
I
thought.

I woke up
this morning,
tired from sleeping, yet not
moving till noon,

Rising

to pretend I'm
an active member of
society.

Sleep living
my way to the outside,

where my greatest
accomplishment of
the day was not
choking on a Twinkie,

unlike the rest of the
fat food-whores of
America.

As a matter of fact,
I didn't even
eat today, though
not by choice.

Boy, I wish
I had a choice
though because
I would have
feasted

(after all, I
never denied
I
was one of
those food-whores)

and acted like I
wasn't
a burnt out moonchild,
broke as hell

because of
institutionalized education
and beyond
the stars job
market.

I would have had
a day like
I was God!

So thank you so
much for that
God-given revelation.

But I think I
heard that gospel
sung today while
I missed
my train
down in the subway.

Thanks for the heads
up though.

And Jesus said,
You're welcome
inside my head.

The Ways We Ask For It

take one:

they say we always ask for it. acting one way, then freaking out when they treat us exactly the way we have been acting.

it was a staircase in one of nine buildings that made up the landscape of my first campus. it was a boy who took me into the backseat of his car several times before for the very same thing. it was the one time i wanted kisses from his lips, not to be kissing between his thighs. it was the first time his voice took on a growling cadence *you know you want it, come on, just a little bit.*

it was the first time i felt my head pressed hard against the wall. it was a sour taste slipping awkwardly between my lips, a twist of the neck. it was the slither of head against my teeth as he stepped back a little too far and i took the opportunity, quickly rambled down the stairs. it was a flapping exit, a sprint to the next building on campus. it was climbing the stairs to a second-floor classroom so i could watch him leave the other building and walk to his car.

it was a blind walk to the bus and finding a seat in the back to huddle in. it was a call to a mutual friend who spoke to me for half the trip home. he kept saying *you'll be okay*, not in words, but by staying near. it was climbing into bed early, no dinner, no nothing, just claims of a headache.

i didn't write sex poems for nearly two years.

take two:

they say we always ask for it. acting one way, then freaking out when they treat us exactly the way we have been acting.

it was a staircase in one of nine buildings that made up the landscape of my first campus. it was a boy who took me into the

46

backseat of his car several times before for the very same thing. it was the one time i wanted kisses from his lips, not to be kissing between his thighs. it was the first time his voice took on a growling cadence *you know you want it, come on, just a little bit.*

it was the first time i felt my head pressed hard against the wall. as his belt buckle fumbled a dance between his fingers, i lifted my foot and pushed against his knee, causing him to become unbalanced.

i quickly went down two flights of stairs before i screamed out *next time he comes out, i'll bite it and i will be spitting a piece back out. don't you ever fucking get near me again!*

i walked to the bus. i found a seat in the back. i took out a notebook and started to write about cutting sausages.

Beatitudes of a Lingering Dystopia

As she made me cry
in the ruins of childhood,
scattered on top
of an ancient television set
—the box filled with 76 winters.

Luckily, those memories floated
back into the clouds,
the basement door swelled
from the storm.

Cherry blossoms arrived
as if on cue,
her diaphragm uncaged.
She'd only remember green
—open-mouthed seed, bearing
a name in the dead
kingdom of Eden.

Emotive Tender

Rust filled her
quiet, morning mouth.
Her ears filled
with disguised voices.
Nose bright, raw
falls to mouth.
Train conductor muffled.
She needs tuning.

Lips feel numb.
It's the stroke.
It's the fear
of falling coins.
Everything is blood,
once it leaks.
Tuesday mornings know
nothing of Sundays.

This Judas of a body
remembers.

You graduated half
moon wishes
to denial, another
winner to head.
I have finally cracked
the code.

I'll have to answer
bloody, mouthed.

Poster Child of Magdalene

Love does not want this body, this falsehood looking for resurrection in eyes that reflect her as altars. Love wants the classic centerfold, not the poster child of the Magdalene complex with numerous notches in her inbox. Love has been deceived by smudges across the screen, the pretend of desire grown by distance. If Love moved closer, Love would see that this body houses nothing but fiction and their story will eventually end. No one falls for the one already on their knees.

I call bluff on the art of letting go.

I've been told you can't kiss a haunting on the lips unless you are ready to carry it to the apotheosis of sainthood. I've been told my eyes carry a devotion no man can look into for fear of drowning. The look, touch, the register of one's soul is enough to collapse your own marrowed-deities. Imagine when it takes shape of inhaled ghosts called memory. Imagine how often the roof of your mouth shakes. In rehab, we call this denial—how to swallow the alphabet backwards as we shape-shift into beings that allows joy to paint caricatures of our pain on our faces, a mask to comfort others.

Drift

Small memory,
go take a walk on
white knuckled
islands.

You're an outlaw
on a gypsy piano,
mapping out
blank tongues
on the back
of glaciers,

floating past
ancient astronauts
on your way
to civilization.

Who told you
the moon was
your child,
when you haven't
seen the sun?

I was told
standing in silence
was not
the way stories
get written.

Wisdom

her hands are permanently stained
with the road maps of birth.

Her occupation?

She delivers breech births of rotten pearls
from the mouths of patrons
getting off on their own bitterness.

Handled with care, she strings each with strands of her hair
until she is covered with
the dull glow of tainted misconceptions
as if each soft, broken inch was a part of her skin.

On her tombstone, it will read:

here lies a woman who took on
every piece of wisdom,
except her own.

Puzzle: Silence

The act of poetry. The pulse of melodies blown under fingertips. The beloved's seconds of veraciousness wrapped in kisses shot directly into jarred skin. The husband's unrelenting pilgrimage to remain in hesitant veins. Flipping through poured pages that break me and make me struggle for my next breath. The struggle between scratching the pen and the breakthrough of rattling syllables. Being in a constant state of creation. Pillows that allow my head to sink lower than the horizon. Bursts of autumn air while looking at sunshine filtered through clouds. Steaming mugs of chai, tainted with vanilla and memory. the extinct stories of my family tree swinging longing into a knot of the debilitating mind of my grandmother. the laughter of womanhood, honeycombed for and against me. meshing edges of my tongue with the decadence of future decay. the creak of a door opening inside of my head. the silent continuous shift of this cognizance sitting in my skin infinitely.

Phases

I am
purple drums
beating
to
the smirks of opening
acts that have nothing
to do with the play,
a forward of Ara
humming Dawn Richard
while meeting you
in panties, Converses
and breasts, loaded
pistol to the hips.

I am
the teacher
with
the ranch-styled
house, cat, bicycles
in driveway,
bananas on counter,
canned corn next

to the sack of potatoes
and ham for dinner,
switching on ABC 7
for Grey's Anatomy,
tweeting quotes
from my iPhone.

I am
a jug of water
mixed
with nitrogen,
a long and lingering
secret love in
Helvetica Bold
under autumn leaves
in Queens,
a cup of tea
tucked between
a stack of literary
magazines and
poetry by Amber Tamblyn.

Mad Gowns

Your mother is a mad
               wedding gown, defiant
in a pantsuit and high collar blouse,
yet complacent
               in dreams of white
picket fences and strollers.

She goes to City Hall
               with a Brooklyn boy promise,
poses for pictures
               in a sweltering Bushwick kitchen
on an October, Indian summer day,
               kissing her heartbreak in the mouth.

Do her cheeks
               become acquainted with
his knuckles before or after the ring?

Does his power
               become a back-handed bullseye
during courtship or after
               the license is signed?

The future is a divided kiss, lined with
               the only hands she has known
to make her tremble
               in qualm or in exaltation,
until one day she birthed passion's broken curse:

you, a new witness
>to her desecration,
you, the path
>to her salvation,
you, the basket
>to place her burdens,
you, the vessel
>for all of her fears,
you, the one
>she shackles with insecurities,
you, the gas light
>she flickers in grief.

You try to quell
>the brokenness in men
who storm like your father,
>kissing heartbreak in the mouth
to distract the curling of their fists.

When you come up for air,
>your mother's reflection stares
back at you, wondering
>if you'll have to fight
her ghosts until you slip on
>your own gown.

Generations: La Familia

father:

he watched his father
weaken the land of his mother
over bowls of arroz y gandules.

he slapped her face
she slapped sazón,
both tenderizing
alimento para los niños.

my father only did what
he was taught, open palm
against my mother

giving her money to
cook a pernil.

Mother:

she watched her mother
as she spoke to the cops
stopping by on Atlantic Avenue.

él es un hijo de puta
trampa y voy a cortarlo.

knives narrowly missing
pop's head as she watched
saturday morning cartoons,

waiting for afternoon
where mr. softee granted
credit for a tribe of eight.

she'll visit him in the land
of coqui and scorpions years
later, remembering how
he narrowly missed a knife.

she will not ask him
to rescue her from creatures
as she stands her ground,
shaking with the kitchen knife.

her mother knew in
San Juan, the cowards will
keep on crawling.

daughter:

she was scared
to scribe all
the tragedy,
kept it locked
in her head.

she watched him
beat her
both eyes swollen shut
after she sent chairs
swinging in
curses.

her pen is her path
to their histories
they foolishly
put in a child of ten.

they did not teach
her spanish, so she snuck
it in as a ghost
at kitchen tables.

grandmothers with
tongues of swords
swiftly retold
tragedies in an alphabet
she struggled to
master,

thinking *la nena*
would never
learn patterns if
she was a little more
gringa instead of
boriqua,

never realizing
that she squeezed
herself between
the muñecas
and rocking chair

soaking in
flailing hands
and
broken hearts
to skipping needles
of Hector Lavoe
and Celia Cruz.

years later
her late night
feelings
boiled down

to everything
she learned from
home sweet home,

the only prayer
she can roll
off her tongue
as she shook
with the possibility
of history repeating:

dame la fuerza
para encontrar un
beso en este mundo.

An Inventory of Your Omentum

You carry your father's habits
underneath the curtains of your omentum,
hoping to stop the infection of
your mother's impuissance.

You've seen your phone flash
with missed calls from a jail cell,
but you *deny deny deny* that
you are worst as their hybrid.

Drugs land you a sentence so you might
go down easier written as a liquid addict.

Bottle, bottle on the floor,
whose memory did you kick out the door?
Bottles scattered in boxes,
under beds, in your vagina,
but you got it under control, right?

Hold on there fancy child,
don't you see your gut growing?
You're carrying too much
rejection in your lymph nodes,
stuffing down your want, need,
want, need because you think
everyone sees the witch in you:

The nothing-good-comes-out-of a girl
who brands her liver with wine sales
and club shots, hoping to magically
bottle pin-prickles of love to cure
the loneliness filtering in her stomach.

Dot

On the anniversary of your expulsion / I visit the church for a mixture of penance / and breath, offering a streak of grief / over the station of flames of the Madonna Della Strada / The moment I enter, I see the crimson mouths of the idols / passion-tide veils to cover the sorrows of the mother I renounced / as a practice and a title / despite memorizing the grainy shape of a heartbeat I couldn't keep / out of desperation / I was raised out of desperation and my back still curves in habit / of being my mother's crutch / I refused to hit repeat while my axis was still trying to find / how to balance the damage / I refused to bear a circumstance instead of an altar / of love between bounds of flesh that have grown away from each other / I loved you, but I worshiped fear and fear / told me the currency of a half-love with the seed that formed you / equals a death I didn't want to form in the flesh / better to drain you into crimson before you formed hands / that would touch my rib cage and pull me into forever / tethered to all the ways I would disappoint you / I loved you as I sat with pills pressed to the side of my cheeks / the choice of a prolonged ruin over the stirrups of an empty-handed standard procedure / I cried over porcelain blemished / with the eyes you'll never form / On the first anniversary I sat / pulling the skin on the back of my hands / the second, you met your grandfather in a zion I am / too numb to enter / and now I kneel in front of the covered face of la madre unbosoming / a grief I don't have permission to claim

Meanwhile,

a dandelion floats
through air, pieces fall
unto concrete, spreading
itself thin as it spins.

She felt the last
petal split along
her cheek, not knowing
where it came from.

She looks up, knowing
he is gone.

Remains

On her neck, a sliced bone, a relic of an old god
dangles above her right hand, waiting to be cremated.

The deadweight of their yesteryears arch her towards
submission; she defiantly keeps her knees above water.

I don't want to remember your name, she prays to a former
life, *I only want to be baptized in what remains without a memory.*

Grief forms a body that can never be cindered,
a replacement of every left that hasn't been right.

And a god dwells on in a place that can't be burned.

Oracular Spectacular

Time to pretend.
That's what weekend wars were about.

Youth, electric kids of the 4th dimensional transition,
telling pieces of what childhood looked like
in the tongues of moons, birds and monsters,
haunting your dreams until you agreed to
reluctantly give up your toy chest.

Handshakes at the dinner table seal the deal
to future reflections of missing important tree house meetings,
not lending your pal your comic books for the weekend
and saying no to sleepovers due to homework.

How long have you yearned for Saturday morning cartoons?

To have the screen so close to your face,
mesmerized by the electric feel radiating
towards the tip of your nose, instead of
touring a photo album of Saturday mornings of
long ago over a morning cup of coffee.

How long has it been?

Sources of Rays

I.

When I come home
    with his belongings,   I'm stuck
    with everything   on top
        of my closet.
In the dark, even paper's
haunted, his pulsating whisper

           of a ghost

challenging my shivers to death

II.

Mami always wears shades

           at night,

    a disguise everyone knows
           at night,
when the luminosity of her   paranoia
           walks

the streets.   UV latex ink   under nails
carry the scent of cheap vodka, the reflection,
    a frothy can
        of [bud] light

III.

The tableau of clouds and
        blues above   the examination
    table glows   I can't bear
    the thought of staring
    at them   for another hour
           give me the pills

IV.

Through the streams   of stinging water,
    I see the stain   of a god
                                   fracturing

V.

Every time I step on stage,   the daunting task
    of transformation is   left to
                                 the ego

    of the spotlight

VI.

The blue light   framing the outline
      of my eyes   as I enter
      another contest   to be denied

VII.

Lake Shore Drive is   a   blur
  of zipping headlights,   of braking
  red, lulling the slant of   eyelashes closed to
           the end,   all roads   ahead

Audacity

one day
the audacity of my being
will mean something.

mark here if you think
you knew me before:

[x].

good.

i like to keep track
of who limits me.

stay tuned

for my coming.

Knees in The Garden

Flowers over job;
spit shine over
taunt skin
of sunflower petals
against the velvet
of my kryptonite
mouth, waiting
to be offered a bouquet
of bushland to graze
along my cheek.

You are beautiful
as you look towards
heaven. I am
your God, right?

As long as
you give me
a garden.

Mother Tongue

Amante,

        let me meet you

on the land of

        my mother tongue,

scrub away

        inconsistencies of city life,

that bears us

        no wishes of

mangoes y plantains.

let me sing you

        lullabies in the language

crossed off and

        scribbled on school desks,

rolled around

        young, unfledged tongues

of lovers looking

        to impress the shaking skin of

wide-eyed

        princesses not ready for

arrows of the beloved,

        el amado.

Le Duc

We wander
warmly through our
private catacombs.

I inhaled
the night under
the collar
of her dress.

She smiled
a martyr's smile
for her own
benefit

a fire
that solitude
presses
against my lips.

Things left
unspoken,
angels ripped
from wombs—

I walk without
flinching through
the burning
cathedral of
the summer

—the squid in
my guts
shuddered.

Coffee Hour and Street Fairs

The pages of the book were scattered into blackholes of rainbows milling about on clouds of rippling soda cracker manmade cotton candy sticky sweet obscenities into californication on her tippy toes where restroom romps told in the pages of the book of pleasantries hide in the attic throwing pillows in evening light manifesting red light specials in the shops of downtown Brooklyn where coffee scented dreams of jurisdiction lay in their yellow pages in the book of neighborhood musicals that cannot get to sleep tonight because no one cut the cake or smeared it on her hips under the black light for sale with the Jimmy running underfoot of rising gas prices in a locket hanging heavy off the pages of the book of Christmas cookies sugared like apple cider donuts smeared on his eyelids like a super fox leaning over the railing of an airport cocked into position seeding into orange pulp spit out over easy rituals for this Thanksgiving feast talked about in the book where my mind commits suicide over the fact that reality had it coming on the 10 o clock news while screaming here is sausages no hot dogs allowed in this mess of bongos beating out the call of the sane in Chiclet sized bibles overworking the pages of the book in favor of lunatics to be a single subject in erotic novels where the cheese gets the girl and leaves its scent on her for wolves to circle around in clown cars making paper cut tattoos on the navels of young banana peels slipping into something more submissive in broad daylight waiting for the chance to kneel in jello saying hello this is nice to be in a caravan of professors waiting to feed us the light of conformity at its worst looking its best in the disguise of consumer products on the shelves twinkling in the eyes of nowhere

Movie Night

If I can't have you, I don't want nobody baby...

Really?

The nights you spend
chasing vodka-soaked
vaginas with lines
of coke on the can
during Thank God It's Fuck-day
doesn't convince me
you spend your nights
pining for me

You pine
for those who open
wide for your thermometer,
wondering how deep is your
love as you check for
that Saturday Night Fever

I don't need to spend
another moment in your
disco inferno

Bare Bones

Damn the circumstances!
You can't do me
with love *and* treachery.

I must be saved on
the tongue of
Our Lady of Pigalle,
instead of running
through the veins of homeless
happiness.

To love you all over again
would be somethin' grand,
licking the river of tears
off my cheeks
and off the palms
of my hands.

Music Lessons

strum me.
callous your fingers
on my rigid back.

you know
the curve of my derrière
as you push down
on
the small of my back
screams at you

to pound and
drop melodies
on my convulsing skin.

we push and pull
our nerves in a tug of war
that
makes love
a casualty in this

whirl of plucking,

blowing orgasms
across hidden intentions

letting them seep into our
pores
like air,
tightening our skin
a moment before
we stretch
and
crack the surface,

releasing the note
found only in arched backs
and
never along guitar strings:

O

76

Sunken Ships

Sticky bun heart of contempt, a drizzle
of honey caught in between sweet fingers
and doughy pitchforks to poke and sizzle
between thoughts of a non-love that lingers

for sadistic scrawlings on salty wounds
and shouts from a heart that saves skin and hu-
miliation under nails by the pounds
for red cheeks and quiet souls that turn blue

Shall we dance in this pool of confusion?
Beating flows from ruptured valves swim at our
feet, rushing pieces of collected allusions
to the soles, ready to puncture and scar

while we hold hands until we fall in love...
is this the ecstasy lovers speak of?

Bear Witness

my mind bears the imprint
of his false heart's history.
no kiss or holy war of
tears can make him disappear.

i live with his denial
through hidden tequila
bottles and numb nights,
but i don't know how to bear

witness to my heart
puckered and scattered
across Southern Brooklyn

and his lies flyblown
to the steps of
my Queens home.

Choices

This is the year I choose to be lonely.

No more loose tongues on West 4th.
No more liquid courage to cure my ails.
No more late-night texts buzzing in my ear.
No more pulling you into corners,
straining my eyes to find your light in the dark.

I cut off all ties from what ifs, if onlys, and semi-regrets.
I will not depend on you to fill the hours.
I won't look for your meaningless banter.
I will stand by myself on street corners and
wait for the sun to graze my cheek instead.

I'll take long walks on Coney Island Avenue and
buy myself a bouquet of flowers for every day you did not.
I'll pick up new habits, bury myself in new hobbies.

I'll take up knitting—

search for every color you bruised my heart.
I'll stitch up bundles of soft yarn around
this discarded body you left a long time ago.
I'll warm up this plush heart, these yearning limbs,
point at myself in the mirror, whispering every day
"You need to sweat her."

I'll keep myself warm morning, noon, and night.

This is the year I choose to love me.

Driving to Chicagoland

Pennsylvania gave us
rest stop kisses,
chicken wings,
and laughs about Victory
pursuing southwest Jewish
boys of Brooklyn.

There were no kisses
on the Ohio Interstate
as toes crossed
snow covered fields,
pushing icicles to
corners of Indiana.

We got a little tipsy
underneath
a patch of stars,
clarity far from
the reach of this city
girl willing
to stick her neck out to
catch a gust of road
in between her lips.

Swedish Sphinx: The Wikipedia of Garboism, A Cento

Flesh and the Devil...
    worlds turned on her movements.
Her instinct, her mastery
    over the machine
        was pure witchcraft.

Gimme a whiskey,
        ginger ale on the side,
        and don't be stingy, baby.

Industry standard,
  my heart will break
        under her.

This time I rise...
        and fall...alone.
I never look ahead.
    By next spring
I shall probably be...
        quite alone.

Time leaves traces
on our small faces and bodies.
      It's not the same anymore,
    being able to pull it off.

I never said, 'I want to be alone';
 I only said, 'I want to be left alone'
      There is a world of difference.

In a few days, it will be the anniversary
            of the sorrow that never leaves me,
that will never leave me
            for the rest of my life.

We cannot help our nature,
        as God has created it,
but I have always thought
        you and I belonged together.

Sunday, Boiling

you gently press me against the wall
like a kid finger painting, no regard
to cover up costs, guests coming over
in twenty minutes, or how loud you
make me scream in furious passion.

i draw maps on your stomach with my breath
skin damp with summer and laziness,
salty from spending our time working out
our hips and spider limbs.

my hair is still damp as the spaghetti boils over.
your parents are downstairs with fresh flowers.

Evolution

You two are bitter
atoms,
tapped from tips of hotel
cigarettes
in moonshine,
falling
into one another,
pooling illusions of
a transparent
heat
birthing a consuming
love, tearing open
the sirens of infinity,
the drink of philosophers,
now
emptied into seasoned mouths.

Jas on the day you break your heart

It's nice that she recognizes
you from behind—
a mailbox full of tears,
locked out of your landfill
where ice cream cartons
and pictures of almost
zombie heartbeats await
to be stains on your pillow.

One look at her face,
I knew.

C: You didn't get Oprah today.
J: I might be getting fired.

I check my phone, but
all I see is whiteness.
It's never been so silent.
I turned around to head
to management, before
I managed to realize,

me too.

/ˌrēyo̅o̅ˈnīt/

v.

Close proximity to him was dangerous. Miles of other people's lives never stopped the occasional ache, but filling their holes with other people's fingers kept it at bay. A rim of tequila and a broken gate on 42nd Street brought rain to her knees, the gun pressed to her cheek in a bathroom stall of headlights. She's a big girl now, so she tossed her tongue indifferently between his cracks. Sensing the tiniest measure of feelings, nostalgia turned quickly into silent contempt. Desire was the switch, but addiction was the God that never left between her ears.

His name gasped everything.

Gospel

don't tell me to god fuck myself when you have already fucked me. my border, my mirror, my hemisphere, my *everything* i've wanted to give you. you are a cop out. you are such a fucking manuscript. you want to take a timetable out for yourself? *oh* i wish we *all* had the luxury. i'm in your face telling you how much i want you and you need to take a break from something you barely dipped your tongue in. *afraid*? guess what?! i am *terrified*. you kissed me. you changed my wound. i wasn't completely happy, but i was surviving. i knew sweetness. i knew his magnitude. but now i know your tradition. now i know your peaks into the routine of loving me. just *love me* damnit. make all of this goddamn suffering worth something. i'm breaking his hemisphere in order not to broadcast yours and all i am doing is breaking my own damn hierarchy. i want to be your gospel. i want to be *yours*. the writer keeps telling me that he's no good, but they have never seen your curiosity. they have never seen you hold world in hand as if all you need is *this* writer. once upon a time we sat on the steps of a bakery and you sang *three little birds* in my ear. i felt like i was your worship. you held me *that* close. which makes this latest demise hurt so much more. you basically condemned me to go fuck your world.

We Talk
Remix of Jewel's We Talk

we talk

slowly
about nothing

we stick to
the surface
and find no
meaning
no substance in
hotel rooms
i used to
unwrap you

now
we are cool
and recount
as though
the sum of our
uses
equaled
something
(more)
substantial

while softer
things shrivel
and dry

go unfed
strangled
and all
that is
not said

Thirst

Today as it rains, I open the door to confront the air of desire. The salt of rain-kissed skin makes my lips yearn for a memory I want to relive but haven't created. I close my eyes and take in the scent of your conjured mouth, flashes of an ache I force to the back of my mind. I don't want you this way, a thirst held in novelty. I want to lay in the grass and talk about the history of what pours out of you. Watch laughter reach your eyes, dig my hands into the real estate of your raptures and ruins. I want to know you. Not you colored in twisted sheets or you glossed over as a swirl of a love potion. I want to know you as a history, to earn a place to kick back and vibe. The scent of rain reduces me to a fleeting hunger, straddling a spectrum of compulsion I need to box away and cross off as a fool's paradise. Who am I to want you as rain?

Falling in The Internet

Miraculously,
the wind tunnel
your voice travels
through stops
behind glass.

I can drown on
the other side without you
seeing my chest
rise in cadence
with your syllables,
begging my brain
to keep my lips
balanced,
from slipping
a sonant praise
of want.

Sometimes my brain
commits beautiful
mistakes without
my permission,
pushing out feelings
before they settle into
a linear path of rationale,
going heartlong
into the wild of falling
in the internet,
with the best version
of you.

Grasping the Mirage

you grew on the nectar of a mirage,
      a study in the rumination of hours as pastime,
      a burgeoning bedroom tongue
      carrying a constant tether to one another.

i want to be the crown to your instant.
      the smirk of the ah-ha of your eyebrows.
      the split second to your hull of cravings.
      our laughter is currency for butterflies born of refuse.

i want you in a vacuum of uncertainty.
      my ego wants your reciprocation, a fool's moon
      of benediction as the ink to the Aesop in my head
      falling in the vicinity of kindred soft spots.

i want to grasp you in carafes of psalms,
      an episode of being dusk of scripture
      written in the ego of a wayward woman,
      spinning around the fable of a madhouse infatuation.

¿te conjuro la soga de un idioma que solo nosotros entendemos o la soledad de tirar un bolígrafo?

In between

No soy un lenguaje secreto
with lips pressed against your neck.
I sweep up goosebumps
con la lengua de una bruja,
worshiping each hitch
arrastrando hacia el sur
until I take in a hymn,
mi boca envuelta en el hechizo de tu virilidad
—another passage pressed to knees,
llevando la memoria de tu piel.

Dear Person: Epistle #1

Dear V.,

You slipped in quietly, in the middle of a no-name day. Sat in the corner, humming a beck and call held closely in your mouth, a tune I follow through the corner of my eye. Your uncertainty is curious but unfocused. I step closer, give you permission to let me down with your proposal; a broken record of offering a rundown tenement of your body—I've heard this pitch before.

I am offered kingdoms for a pledge of my submission on a regular basis.

We briefly tease out the game, circle around intrigue. Too quickly, we retreat back to our corners of the earth and go on as if nothing passed our lips. I watch from a distance, unsettled. Something inside me keeps bubbling thoughts I push away. Through all the ordinary things I don't want to say, lies a muse fiddling with the matchbook, using her head to scratch the surface I wish to burn. I bite my tongue and refuse to form a god out of my curiosity of you.

You're the first altar I don't want to adorn.

On paper, there is no way we would blend. If we were total strangers, we would probably pass each other. Adonis does not carry on with Eve until after she takes a bite of the apple to prove her sin. I won't deny the urge to trail kisses from your Adam's apple down to your snakehead, but I've performed this act of carnality before. I don't want to apologize for a fleeting moment and have it mistaken for love.

Especially, when I want to know...

I can't explain the urge to know more than a glance. From afar, I see you in angles I am curious about. What's your history? Your passion to move in the world? What makes your eyes crinkle in laughter? Your heart drop in fear? What are your favorite stories? How many times have you fallen in love? Who makes up your family? What's your favorite meal? Your favorite secret? Guilty pleasures? What...

makes me care so much?

I could have you in ungodly ways, knee-to-lip benediction, a worship that would blow our minds for a night. I could burn in a love that would never ignite a flame, leaving a wreckage of wanton regret. Yet all I want is your vibe, to see your humanity, to complete a history I wanted to know when my moon was still rising.

I know you are probably not interested in giving away more than a boyhood curiosity. Lackluster encounters should dampen the compulsion to chit chat myself into a deeper connection. You're a classic lesson in "people make an effort for those they want to spend time with." One-word answers to curve the intentions you don't think of asking about.

I don't want you in the form of love poems and romantic comedies. I don't want you as a smutty magazine or meet-ups in the Red Light District. I'm attracted to the pull of watching you from a distance, to the stories I conjure in my mind about the kindness I see in your eyes. You've triggered a *je ne sais quoi* kind of something.

I'm not brave enough to ask if we can vibe and I know you wouldn't have an interest. I care too much for the average person, an awkward mess of fumbling "How do you do" with apologies for taking up your time. I'm at the age where I don't know how to ask if we can be friends without going through a round of attempted romance. I have to get over this: the overthinking, the oversharing, the over you.

I put this letter into the universe as my final word. I take the hint to bury the need. Personally, I hope this never finds you, that the universe will make it so that you are too busy to notice the foolishness marked down for prosperity. Pardon the need to poem you, that's just who I am. Pardon my heart, it's just too big along with the body that shadows what you could have seen in me. Ignore me as other timelines do. By the time you find this, my eyes will have learned to skip over you and even if that's not the case, let's pretend they have.

Sincerely,

The woman who is learning to turn down her gods

Wildflowers in Your Head

It is not in my nature to bloom within a greenhouse. I am a
wildflower, a weed perhaps. I need open and untamed spaces to
sprout. I need to ask the questions and think the thoughts that
others overlook. —Dawna Markova

...so I am brujería in your garden,
a spell of questions, day after day
—commanding your fingertips
to breathe devotionals.

I make you a gentleman of
inconvenience, tipping
your hat to staged
contradiction you lay
on top of inundated
soft spots for me to cross,

forcing you to bring
hours upon my name
—your poor, poor hands
that pressed the trigger
every time I didn't stare,
the weed you never pull out.

—I Will Not Die an Unlived Life
Copyright © 2000 by Dawna Markoza

Fleeting

I glance at you & become
completely dismantled
by the beauty of eyes eschew to
an overture others pray for

a vice, knees, a mouth, worship

a limited run to erupt the curios,
circle around the corporeal
of fulfillment, tug of war
on arousal vs. emotion

deny, push, my pride, pull

back to the first line
of contact, I swallowed
the boundary between a bygone
era, granting a flood

a tease, veins, the nerve, in vain

Unfinished

Your young heart is always tucked away in the corners of an adult cage. Holding flashbacks to hours spent at the keyboard. The back and forth of budding sexuality. The love of pulling him closer with each exchange. Desperate longing building against a swelling screen. Plans made, waiting till the walls are empty of gatekeepers. Sneaking around bed sheets, the folds spread to allow entry, ready to be torn into womanhood. Unsuccessful attempts to bring down the virgin, resistant of the battering ram. Defeated by skin unyielding. A resignation. Scrambling to gather bits of clothes. The click of a lock, the panic shoved into the closet to avoid the flame. Caught and captured, thrown and banished. Fairy tale interrupted. Young love collapsed into a checkbox of "not worth it."

A young flower wilted.

I used to wonder where time hid him. A faint twinge of teenage desire, fading into the stream of triumphant limbs. Nearly forgotten till one day, an appearance. I step forward in conversation. Check. Months later, he steps forward in a veiled request. Checkmate. Do you let a yesteryear love darken your frame? Grip the hands of the clock until you're spent and breathless? Lead strangers of a half-grown life from behind the screen once again, letting versed hands orchestrate an unfinished scene? Not this time. Let it be implied, fate decides the next time the plane touches down.

The secret garden is yet to bloom.

Notes on Previous Publication

- Querencia Press' Not Ghosts, But Spirits Vol II, "Grasping the Mirage," "Le Duc," "Remains," "Beatitudes of a Lingering Dystopia," "Prize: Fat Girl," 2023
- Querencia Summer 2022 Anthology, "Mad Gowns," 2022
- Close Up: Poems on Cancer, Grief, Hope and Healing, "Sources of Rays," edited by Orchard Lea Books, 2022
- Satin Soulbits, "In between," "Poster Child of Magdalene," 2019
- War Crimes Against the Uterus, "Dot," edited by Wide Eyes Publishing, 2019
- She Will Speak Series: Gender Based Violence Anthology, "Generations: La Familia," edited by Cheyenne Jacobs of She Will Speak, 2019
- Tupelo Quarterly i.8, "Daily Bread," 2015
- The Body Narratives, "Wisdom," "Puzzle," 2013
- Old Hollywood, "Swedish Sphinx," edited by Shannon Lynette, 2013
- A Thing Of Beauty Painted By Words, "Generations: La Familia," edited by Caits Meissner, 2013
- Skeletons, "Wisdom," "Confessions," edited by Shannon Lynette, 2013
- Other Rooms Press i.8, "An Inventory of Your Omentum," 2011
- Yes, Poetry, "Music Lessons," 2011
- rust + moth, "Sunken Ships," 2011
- amphibi.us, "Oracular Spectacular," "Movie Night," 2010

Acknowledgments

I am forever grateful to the press that gave my book a home. Querencia Press and editor Emily Perkovich made a dream come true. I was always prepared to do this myself. I am not afraid of self-publishing and the work it takes. But to have someone who believes in my work? I can't start to put into words what this means to any writer. Thank you, thank you, thank you Emily and Querencia Press for believing in me.

To all the literary magazines and presses of anthologies who gave individual poems their first place in the world. Thank you for giving them light.

To my parents, Iris and Dennis Rodriguez. I know you don't always understand the path that is my life, but you have never discouraged me from pursuing my passions. Thank you for always being a fan, for loving me, for raising me. Mom, you drive me crazy in all the best and worst ways, but it's always been us. Dad, I miss you every day. I hope, somehow, you can see this and are proud.

To my beloved, Alshawn Kelly-Rushing. Our love has grown into a partnership filled with trust, support and a lot of adventure. Thank you for being my best friend.

To my family in everything but blood. As an only child, friends become extended family in a deeper way. Samantha Budhoo, Liz Ramanand, Ali Karimullah, Marisol Cepeda, Simone Malcolm, Amber Davis, Ana Cardenas, Shobhana Bipat, Jessica Irvin, Annette Estévez, Kristy Roberts, Alex Scelso/Sitanya Face, Deryck Khusial, Phil Kellerman, Dan Moran, Demetrious Lyon and many more whom I have bonds with. Thank you for being my family, for always seeing me in ways I don't see myself. Your love and support mean the world to me. I found a quote that has been credited to no one, that fits the bill: "A friend is one who overlooks your broken fence and admires the flowers in your garden." Thank you for loving my garden.

To my family, especially my tio William De Los Santos, my titi Nilsa Santos, and my cousin Melissa De Los Santos. Thank you for your love, your belief in me, and for your excitement for my dreams.

To my AMA work family, Leah Strauss and Ivonne Cueva, thank you for being excited for me and this book. Your support means the world to me. To Brande Martin, whose belief in my professional life gave me the courage to continue striving in my creative life. You'll always be my favorite boss. To all my other colleagues who know about this book, thank you for your support.

To those who have nurtured my poetry and writing through community, through chance and through craft:

To the Chicago Writers Association, our members and my fellow board members, but especially Randy Richardson and Marcie Hill. Your belief in me has let me step into a role in the literary community that I could only dream of. I know whatever I pursue, I have a community behind me.

To Annette Estévez, Alex Scelso/Sitanya Face, Anuradha Bhowmik, Lyn Patterson, Melis Gördem, and Osei Haywood—your friendship as both as poets and great people have kept me going. I don't think I would have kept going as a poet without your inspiration and dedication to the craft. Our journeys together have meant the world to me.

I especially want to shout out Annette for being my soulmate, my sis, by reading poetry with me at bars, our "Solitude and Cough Drops" sessions, and most importantly, for helping me with your eye on my work, especially for this book. You were the first to see many of these poems and the first to see it as a whole. You know some of the stories and histories. You inspire me with your own words and art. You give me sisterhood and love. Without you, writing would be lonely, but also life.

To the Brooklyn College Poetry Club of 2008-2010: You were my first community. I love you all for everything you have brought to my life.

To Daniel Cohen, who saw a lot of these poems come to life. Thank you for all the advice, edits and love you put into my work, and the adventures we had along the way.

Ed Go and Joe Robitaille, who were my professors at Brooklyn College, for sparking and nurturing my poetry/creative writing journey. Thank you for giving me the push to take my writing beyond the classroom.

Thank you to all those I've met—facilitators, students, and friends—at Winter Tangerine, Frost Place, and all the various workshops and communities I've been a part of over the years.

Thank you to my following on social media, especially Instagram, for appreciating and supporting my work, and for sharing your lives with me.

To the past loves, who inspired some of these poems—I regret everything and nothing. Your time in my life taught me many valuable lessons. Thank you for our moment in time.

To the readers of this book, thank you for choosing me to be a part of your shelf and life with these poems. This is all for you.

CPSIA information can be obtained
at www.ICGtesting.com
Printed in the USA
BVHW052256300123
657453BV00010B/127